Professor Bubbles' Official

Bubble Handbook

By Richard Faverty
with John Javna

Greenleaf Publishers, Schenevus, New York

This book is dedicated to my family

Created and Packaged by John Javna
Design by Andrea Sohn
Cover design: Ron Addad and Roland Addad
Illustrations by Michelle Montez and Lonnie Graham

ISBN 0-913-31905-8
First Edition 10 9 8 7 6 5 4 3

ACKNOWLEDGMENTS

I've been playing with bubbles for many years, but I never tried to write about them before. It's a lot harder than it looks.

Fortunately, I had help from some wonderful people in putting this book together. My sincere thanks to:

•**Lyn**, my wife, who let me make bubbles instead of fixing the plumbing.
•**Sandy and Carrie**, who've helped me discover bubbles in my own backyard, and who make pretty good models, too.
•**The Tootsietoys trio—Dick, Mike and Tom Shure**—for their continuing advice and support. This project never would have happened without their help, and I look forward to a long, fruitful association with them.
•**Dean Roberts**, owner of Greenleaf Publishers, the famous philosopher who pointed out that "Life is like a bubble."
•**Bill Quinn**, of Greenleaf.

•**John Javna**, the bald book maniac of Berkeley.
•**Eiffel Plasterer**, for introducing me to the incredible world of bubbles.
•**Harry Brown**, whose counsel in the area of design has been invaluable.
•**Jeff Alward**, who drew Professor Bubbles and was generous with design advice.
•**M.J. Murphy, Renny Mills, Michelle Byrne**, and **Kati Rooney**, for photographic assistance way beyond the normal limits of endurance.
•**Andrea Sohn**, who designed the superb interior pages.
•**John Schutz** and his sales staff at Tootsietoys, for taking this project to heart.
•**Rick Heeger** at Custom Process Photo Labs in Berkeley, for his timely suggestions and for bringing Javna good luck.
•**Joel Copeland** and **David Reinisch**,

for their video expertise.
•**Bruce Fritz**, a fantastic photographer & a terrific friend and advisor.
•**Diane Sautter**, of the Expressways Children's Museum, a steadfast supporter.
•**Ron Addad and Roland Addad**, who designed the cover.
•**Sal Murillo**, for helping me get started performing.
•**Anice Hall**, for her retouching.
•**All our models**, who are literally too numerous to mention in the space left. You're all wonderful, and made the book fun to look at. Not bad bubble-ologists, too.
•**Lonnie Graham** and **Michelle Montez**, for beautiful illustrations
•**All the hardworking production people.**
•**Lynn Schneider** and **Bob Migdal**
•**Co-op Type (Elania, Jay, Doug)**
•**Kevin McGarvey**
•**Gideon** and **Sam Javna** and **Sharon**.

CONTENTS

INTRODUCTION

From Kodak film to Bubble film

Although I perform under the name "Professor Bubbles," my real name is Richard Faverty. For many years, I've been a professional photographer in Chicago.

In fact, that's how I fell in love with soap bubbles. Back in 1980, I received an assignment from a national magazine to photograph them. I was astounded by their beauty, and soon I began experimenting with bubbles myself.

This path of discovery led me to Eiffel Plasterer, the world's foremost bubble-ologist. As a photographer, I had only considered the *visual* aspects of bubbles. But Eiffel opened my eyes to other miraculous possibilities. He shared his extensive scientific knowledge and demonstrated many of his fantastic discoveries.

But even more important, he passed on his enthusiasm. It was as if "bubble fever" was contagious. Mr. Plasterer was so completely caught up in bubbles that by the time I left, I could hardly think of anything else.

My fascination grew from there. Within a week, I had figured out a way to enclose my daughter Sandy inside a giant soap bubble. And within a month, I was spending every spare moment mixing bubble solution, making different kinds of hoops and trays. I made bigger and bigger bubbles, including my largest so far—a bubble 12 feet in diameter.

Since then, I've put in countless hours playing with bubbles, developing techniques and tricks…or just having fun. I've also created a bubble act and taken it to the far corners of the world, entertaining hundreds of thousands of people in person and millions more on television.

I'm still a photographer, but bubbles have become a major part of my life. I believe that there's nothing on Earth which captures the fragile essence of nature's gifts the way bubbles do.

This book is a wonderful opportunity to share what I've discovered and enjoyed over the past seven years.

It's geared to beginners—both children and adults—but I'm sure that every bubble enthusiast will find something exciting in it.

I recommend that you follow the book in order, page by page. It's arranged in order of difficulty, so as you complete each step, you will master a new skill...or get hands-on experience with an important facet of bubble-ology. If you discover you've got a knack for bubbles, you can skim right through the easy ones.

When you've gone through the tricks in this book, take the next step—invent your own. There are too few bubble-ologists in the world right now. We need you to join us.

photo by John Javna

ASK PROFESSOR BUBBLES

Here are answers to some of the questions about bubbles that people frequently ask.

What is a bubble?

Here's how the Lawrence Hall of Science (Berkeley, CA) answers that question in its publication, *Bubbles: Films, Foams and Fizz:*
"A bubble, by our definition, is encapsulated gas. The material that surrounds the gas could be a soap film, or it could be lemon meringue ...When you hold your breath, you become a human bubble."

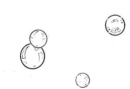

What is the biggest soap bubble ever made?

No one's quite sure, because there's no official record-keeping (Guinness hasn't included it in its book of records yet). However, the largest round one I've ever made was 12 feet in diameter. And the longest was a tube about 30 feet long, by 3 feet wide.

What is the longest amount of time that an individual bubble has ever lasted?

Eiffel Plasterer, the dean of bubble-ologists, specializes in preserving bubbles. He actually keeps them in jars in his bubble laboratory. The longest that Eiffel has kept one is almost a year—340 days! Surely, this is a world's record.

What are the most unusual bubbles ever made?

Three types of bubbles stand out in my mind as the most amazing:
1. Tom Noddy, the famous California bubble-ologist, has devised a way of doing the seemingly impossible—he has created a square bubble.
2. Ilan Chabay, who runs the New Curiosity Shop (consultants in creative science education) in Palo Alto, California, freezes bubbles by blowing them into a plexiglass box with dry ice on the bottom.
3. Eiffel Plasterer, by varying a mixture of hydrogen and oxygen inside a bubble, can either make it go up in flames, or explode with a bang.

If you add dye to bubble solution, will the bubbles come out different colors?

No, it doesn't make any difference what color the solution is—bubbles aren't affected by that.

Then why do we see colors in bubbles?

We see the colors in bubbles through the reflection and refraction of waves of light. The wall of a bubble has 2 surfaces—an outside surface and an inside surface. These two surfaces are only a few millionths of an inch apart, and both of them relfect light back to us just like a mirror. As the waves of light come off of these two surfaces, they interfere with each other—which causes the rainbow-like colors we see.

Why are some bubbles prettier than others?

Because the solution is thicker. The thicker the wall, the more intense the color is.

How popular are bubbles?

Dick Shure, president of Strombecker—the world's largest bubble merchandiser—reports that bubble solution is the biggest-selling toy item in America. Over 50 million containers are sold every year.

Why are bubbles round?

Soap bubbles embody the principle that scientists refer to as "minimal surfaces." Imagine that the wall of a bubble is like a piece of elastic, always pulling inward. The laws of nature say that this elastic will try to enclose the air inside of it with the least amount of surface area possible. As it happens, the geometric form that holds the volume of air with the least surface area is a sphere. That's why bubbles are always round.

Why do bubbles burst?

Here are several reasons why:

1. A collision. When they bump into something—a house, a tree, etc.— bubbles crash and break.

2. Evaporation. The water simply evaporates from the bubble.

3. Deterioration. The forces of gravity, acting on the bubble solution, make the wall so thin that it can't exist any longer.

4. Air pollution and particles of dust.

5. Heavy air turbulence. Wind can literally blow them apart.

Are there many bubble-ologists in the world?

The "bubble community" is still relatively small, although it's growing. Of course, there's no formal designation of "bubble-ologist." But there *is* an informal network of recognized bubble experts who perform at bubble festivals. Since there's little competitiveness in the field, ideas and information are traded freely. As a result, it's easy for people to get involved with bubbles. I have learned a great deal—including some of the tricks in this book—from people who preceded me as bubble enthusiasts. Here's a list of some of the better-known bubble-ologists:

•**Eiffel Plasterer:** The most famous contemporary figure in bubbles, and justifiably so. His work over the last 45 years has become the foundation for most of modern-day bubble-ology. His "Bubbles Concerto" is the premier performance piece in the world of bubbles.

•**Tom Noddy:** A "bubble troubador" who has created many of the very delicate, very beautiful bubble sculptures that are classics today.

•**Bernie Zubrowski:** An educator, museum executive, and bubble enthusiast who has written *Bubbles: A Children's Museum Activity Book.*

•**David Stein:** A New York City architect who invented the amazing Bubble-Thing, a device for blowing huge bubbles.

•**Dr. Ilan Chabay:** Creator of the frozen bubble, a chemistry professor and proprietor of The New Curiosity Shop, and a fantastic source of information about bubble science.

•**Louis Pearl:** One of the most enthusiastic bubble-ologists I've ever met. His Tangent Toy Company manufactures the Bubble Trumpet.

•**Sterling Johnson:** A San Francisco attorney and our chief proponent of "handmade" bubbles.

•**Ze'ev Luz:** Vice President of the Weizmann Institute of Science in Israel, a devotee who avidly demonstrates the physics of bubbles.

Where can I learn more about the science of bubbles?

I've avoided getting technical in this book because I wanted you to concentrate on just having fun with bubbles. But if you really want to understand more about them, I recommend that you start with *The Exploratorium Magazine: Bubbles*, which you can order from The Exploratorium, 3601 Lyon Street, San Francisco, CA 94123. Have fun!

THE RIGHT SOLUTION

As you work your way through this book, you'll be making many kinds of bubbles. It's important to use the right bubble solution for each one.

There is no perfect bubble solution. But depending on what you want from your bubbles—lightness, strength, longevity, etc.—there are different ones to use.

Every bubble-ologist has at least one favorite formula that he or she recommends; I've got three.

Bubble Solution #1

This is the easiest—a jar of Mr. Bubbles ™ bubble solution.

Through my experiments, I've discovered that Mr. Bubbles ™ is the best commercial bubble solution in the U.S.; it makes the longest-lasting *and* the prettiest bubbles. For many of the tricks included in this book, I've used it right out of the jar and gotten impressive results.

The best thing about Mr. Bubbles ™, though, is that you can go to the store, buy a bottle, and you're ready to go—there's no fuss…and it's a guaranteed success.

I enjoy Mr. Bubbles ™ so much , in fact, that I've asked its creator— Tootsietoy—for permission to include their character in this book. They've agreed, so throughout the book, you'll find **"Mr. Bubbles' Tips."**

Science Note: Commercial bubble solution is very light—which is why the bubbles float up into the sky. It's also the reason that the walls of these bubbles are thin. So when you start making bubbles over 10 inches in diameter, you need to add something to thicken them.

Bubble Solution #2

• Start with an 8-ounce container of Mr. Bubbles ™ bubble solution.

Mix in:

• 1 ounce of Dawn or Joy liquid dishwashing detergent. (I've experimented with many kinds of dishwashing detergents—these are absolutely the best).

• 6 ounces of water (preferably distilled, but *not* hard water; that will actually retard the solution).

• 1 ounce of glycerine (pure glycerine, not the kind with rosewater in it). This is available at any drug store. It's a thickening agent that makes the bubble walls last longer.

Notes: Whenever you add Dawn to your bubble solution, you also have to add water. But the quality of water varies everywhere you go. Hard water is very bad for bubble solution. Soft water is much better. And the best water of all is distilled water—which is available at any grocery store.

Save Your Solution

Bubble solution with Dawn (or Joy) and glycerine added to it ages well. In fact, it actually gets better as it gets older. I have bubble solution I've kept for a year at a time.

Mix Your Solution

Many people assume that commercial bubble solution and additives can't be mixed together. Actually, the opposite is true. Combining the two is the easiest way to get sure-fire, quality bubbles that last. Especially for beginners.

Bubble Solution #3

This is the Industrial Strength variety. For super-strong bubbles, add another ounce of Dawn dishwashing detergent. Then keep on playing with the solution, adjusting it as you like.

Performer's Bubble Solution

The bubble solution I use in large quantities is:

• 4 gallons of Mr. Bubbles ™ bubble solution
• 1 quart of glycerine
• 1 quart of Dawn
• 1 quart of water

The Last Word in Solution

There is none. These recipes are simply guidelines to start you off. You should experiment to find the right bubble solution for you, refining it to match the climate and time of year you're working in.

THE BUBBLE WAND

Most people are introduced to the world of bubbles with a simple wand when they're very young....which makes it the perfect tool for us to begin with.

As a bubble-ologist, you'll discover right away that there's more to do with bubble wands than you ever imagined.

But that's not all. By playing and practicing with your wand, you'll also learn to "think bubbles." You'll get a feeling for just how delicate and beautiful they are. And you'll learn breath control and dexterity.

Experimenting with Professor Bubbles' homemade Stone Age bubble wand.

PREPARATION

Materials You'll Need

- Two bubble wands

- Mr. Bubbles TM bubble solution (several bottles, so you have enough fluid and an extra wand).

Note: The best bubble wands to use with this book are about 6-7 inches long, with a single bubble loop.

- The ones with two bubble loops are great for normal bubble-making, but they aren't as good for tricks—you need to keep your hand as far from the bubble as possible.

- Short wands make it hard to handle big bubbles. A 6-inch bubble is already wider than the stem of a short bubble wand, so it tends to fall back into your hand and pop.

Set-Up

You can do these tricks wherever you want, but it's easier to learn them indoors, where there's no wind. If you're outdoors, pick a sheltered spot.

When bubbles pop—especially when you're doing a lot of them—they get the floor a little wet. It's not much, but you still might want to do this in a basement and lay out some newspaper.

TIPS

- Always dip the whole wand—including the stem—into your bubble solution. A dry stem may pop your bubbles.

A bubble-ologists' secret: Bend your wand so it it has a slight *upward* curve to it.

The reason: When you hold a bubble—especially a larger one—on the end of a straight bubble wand, it tends to fall back toward your hand.

If you curve your wand *up,* the bubble will hang freely from the loop.

THE MAGIC WAND

There's something wonderful about blowing bubbles with a bubble wand. Each little bubble is so perfect, so beautiful…and so easy to make! After all these years, I still love to watch them float into the sky.

So before we get into any bubble tricks, let's take the time to loosen up with some good old-fashioned bubble-making.

Open your jar of bubble solution, dip in your wand, and blow….

Bubbles for Sale

In this book, you'll be making bubble tools out of household objects. But don't forget that there are also some wonderful bubble products available in stores. Most are inexpensive, but provide hours of entertainment —which makes them true bargains.

Here's one that I invented—Mr. Bubbles' Swiss Bubble Blower, which has six different bubble wands in it.

The Tootsietoy Lotsa Ways TM bubble package is a great starter kit.

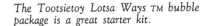

And there's Mr. Bubbles' Million Bubbles, which comes with two wands— one makes lots of bubbles at once, and the other makes a single giant bubble. It also comes with bubble solution, and its own pan.

Other recommended bubble toys:

• **Louis Pearl's Bubble Trumpet** (Tangent Toys, San Francisco) is a big bubble blower that's lots of fun.

• **David Stein's Bubble Thing**, a fantastic wand you can use to make giant bubbles.

THE BASIC BUBBLE

Professor's Notes

To do tricks with your bubble wand, you have to know how to make a bubble that's about 4 to 6 inches in diameter. So that's the first thing we'll learn here. It's the bubble-ologist's basic bubble.

Level: Beginner.

Place: Indoors, or in a sheltered spot outside. A strong breeze will blow your bubble away.

Tips: This may be the first time you ever try to control the size of a bubble with your breath. It's an important step, so take it slowly.

•My favorite place to practice this is over the kitchen sink.

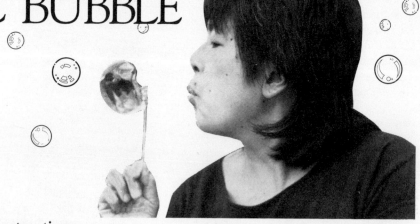

Instructions

1. Dip the bubble wand in the bubble solution. Get the stem wet, too.

2. Hold the bubble wand approximately 8-10 inches away from your face.

3. Blow gently, as if you're exhaling.

The bubble film will begin to fill with air, getting bigger, and bigger…
• Gentle is the key word here. And the further away from your face the bubble wand is (within reason), the gentler the air will be when it hits the bubble film.
• If you hold the wand too close, the force will just blow away the film.

Holding a basic bubble

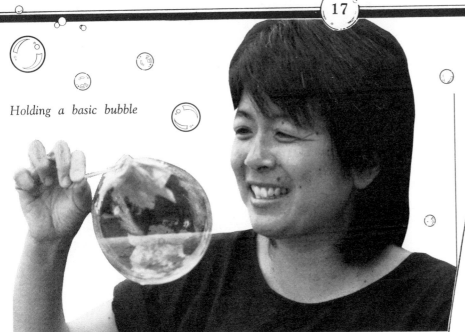

TIPS

• Blowing a bubble is like blowing up a balloon; with a balloon, you have to blow harder at the beginning to start the air flowing—then it's easy to inflate.

• The same is true with the bubble. When you start, you have to blow a bit harder to get the bubble going.

Note: If you blow a lot of small bubbles instead of one big one, either you're blowing too hard or you've got the wand too close to your mouth.

4. When the bubble reaches a diameter of about 6 inches, finish it off with a quick flick of the wrist, and catch it again on the end of the wet wand.

The Secret: Sort of *roll* it over from one side of the wand to the other.

The basic bubble should now be hanging off the bubble wand. Congratulations.

THE DISAPPEARING BUBBLE

When you've mastered the Basic Bubble, you can do this easy "magic" trick.

1. Blow a Basic Bubble. Hold the wand so the bubble is hanging down from it.

2. Say something corny, like, "Watch as I magically make this bubble disappear," and add some "secret words." Ham it up.

3. While you say them, secretly break the bubble film by touching the bubble from the top (through the loop) with a dry finger. Air will seep out of the bubble, slowly deflating it. The bubble will look like it's disappearing!

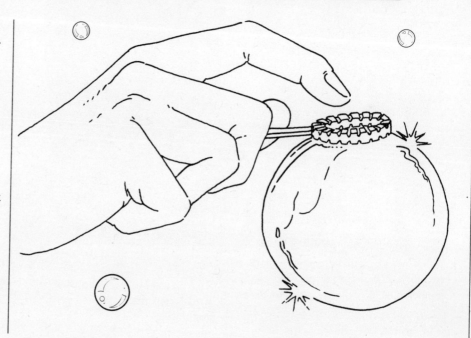

TWIN BUBBLES

Professor's Notes

The next step is to learn to control two bubbles at once.

Mastering this technique opens up all kinds of new possibilities for experimenting with bubbles. It also teaches dexterity.

Level: Beginner.

Place: Anywhere, as long as there's no wind.

Tip: The tough part of this trick is holding on to the first bubble while you blow the second. You have to blow the second bubble fast, because the first bubble will evaporate if you take too long.

Instructions

1. Hold a bubble wand in each hand. Dip them both.

2. Blow a Basic Bubble and catch it on one wand.

3. Make a second Basic Bubble, catch it on the second wand...and you've got a bubble in each hand. Practice holding them, moving them around in front of you, putting one on top of the other, etc.

4. Repeat the whole process a number of times—until you're comfortable with it.

THE DOUBLE BUBBLE

Professor's Notes

After you've learned to work with a bubble in each hand, you're ready to make a double bubble by joining the two together.

Level: Intermediate.

Place: Indoors, or outdoors if there's little wind.

Science: First, bounce the bubbles together at the sides—notice they don't attach; the walls of the bubble will not join together, no matter how much force you use. This is a demonstration of the surface tension in a bubble.

Instructions

1. Follow the procedures for making Twin Bubbles.

2. When you've got a bubble on each of your two wands, bring the two bubbles together.

3. As you touch the bubbles together, take the wet part of one of the

TIPS

People often have trouble holding bubbles on the end of the wands, because they hold the ends of the wands up in the air. Then the bubble floats downward, toward your fingers, touches the dry part of the wand...and pops. **The Solution:** Hold the wand so the end of it is tilted down, with the bubble falling away from the bubble wand. That way, it can't hit the dry part of your hand.

wands and touch it to the wall of the other bubble. The bubbles will "magically" join. It's that easy.

Swinging Bubbles: Making A Threesome

•Once you've got a double bubble, you can just hold it like that, between the two wands, or you can turn the bubble into a "swinger" by removing one of the wands and holding the two bubbles on a single wand.

•**Here's how:** Gently twist the wand and pull it off at the "pointed" part of the surface.

•You can then blow another bubble and repeat the process, joining a third bubble to the chain . And you can keep repeating it until you've got five or six bubbles.

•When you're joining three bubbles together and they accidentally form a triangle instead of a chain, pop one of the bubbles with your finger and start again.

Uncouple the Bubbles

•Now that you've got them together, try pulling them apart. Sometimes this is possible, depending on how big the bubbles are.

•Bubbles always stick to the biggest surface, so if the surface where the bubbles join is bigger than the diameter of the bubble wand, the bubbles will stay together.

•But if they're little bubbles, they can be pulled apart.

•You can also try to make one bubble out of them.

ADVANCED BUBBLE-OLOGY

Professor's Notes

I'm not sure this belongs in the first chapter—it's a lot harder than it looks. On the other hand, it's a good bubble wand trick.

My suggestion: Read this through, give it a try, and then keep going on to the next chapter.

While you're learning other tricks, practice this one, too. Work on it over a period of time...eventually, you'll get it down.

Level: Intermediate.

Place: Indoors, or outside in a sheltered, breeze-free spot.

Instructions

1. Blow a basic bubble

Just "kiss" the bubble gently with your breath.

2. Hold it 8 to 10 inches from your face.

3. Blow gently on the wall of the bubble, "kissing" it with your breath. A second bubble will form out of the wall and appear inside the first one.

• The secret here is in the breath.

• First, there's breath control; you've got to consciously direct your breath to a specific spot on the bubble wall.

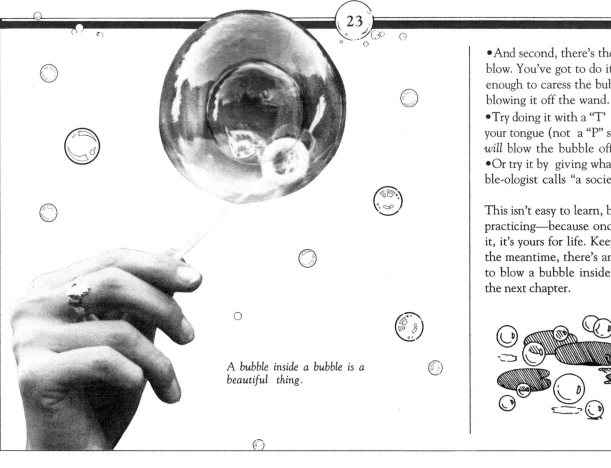

A bubble inside a bubble is a beautiful thing.

• And second, there's the *way* you blow. You've got to do it just easy enough to caress the bubble without blowing it off the wand.

• Try doing it with a "T" sound, using your tongue (not a "P" sound—that *will* blow the bubble off the wand).

• Or try it by giving what one bubble-ologist calls "a society cough."

This isn't easy to learn, but it's worth practicing—because once you master it, it's yours for life. Keep trying. In the meantime, there's an easier way to blow a bubble inside a bubble in the next chapter.

SOAP & STRAWS

The Bubble Burst • Glassblower's Bubble • Expanding Bubble • Bubble Inside A Bubble

"A large soda, and a bubble wand please."

Of course, you've never actually said that...but without realizing it, you've probably ordered it many times in restaurants. That's because every time someone hands you a drinking straw, you're also getting one of the greatest bubble-makers ever devised.

In this chapter, we'll combine the bubble wand you already know how to use, with a new tool—the common straw.

You'll quickly see how using the two together makes bubbles more fascinating.

Using a straw with your bubble wand gives you a whole new outlook on bubbles...and straws!

PREPARATION

Materials You'll Need

•A jar of Mr. Bubbles ™ bubble solution.

•A plastic drinking straw (or several, if you've got them—they get pretty slippery after a while).

•A standard bubble wand.

•Optional: Flexible straws (the ones with ridges that let you bend them at one end). They're more versatile. When you learn to blow bubbles with straws, you can bend a flexible straw and make a bubble pipe out of it.

Set-Up

•You can do these anywhere.

•Outdoors, breezes will make them hard to do. So if you're outside, shelter yourself from the wind.

NOTES

Building Bubbles

•This chapter demonstrates the concept of "customizing" bubbles.

•Even though bubbles are very fragile, it's possible to alter them if you use the proper tools.

•The tools we'll use in this chapter are very simple. But as we go on in the book, we'll add more complicated ones... and do more with them.

THE BUBBLE BURST

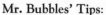

Professor's Notes

When I was young, I loved pea shooters….and blowing bubbles out of a straw like this reminds me of them. There's no other way to make so many perfect little spheres. If you blow several times into a gentle breeze—quickly dipping and blowing, dipping and blowing—all of a sudden, the air is filled with zillions of tiny bubbles. It's an incredibubble sight.

Level: Beginner. Anybody can do it.

Tips: When people first try this, they usually blow too hard through the straw…and then all the solution comes out the end. Instead, blow gently so you don't break the bubble film at the end of the straw.

Instructions

1. Dip the straw in the solution. Get 2 inches at the end of the straw wet.

•Roll the straw a little as you dip it, to make sure it gets wet on all sides. Then, if you need to, gently drain off the extra solution.

2. Exhale gently—very gently—through the straw. You'll fill the air with a stream of tiny bubbles.

Mr. Bubbles' Tips:
Because the straw can't hold enough bubble solution to make very many bubbles, you'll only get one nice burst of them each time. Then you have to dip into the solution again.

GLASSBLOWER'S BUBBLE

Professor's Notes

When you blow through a straw as gently as possible, you get one simple, beautiful bubble at the end of your straw. It's so delicate that it feels a little like you're blowing glass.

Level: Beginner.

Tip: If you don't get any bubbles, it's probably because you've broken the bubble film at the end of the straw, which is very weak. Blow more gently....Or just keep dipping the straw into the bubble solution to create a better bubble film across the end. Remember to rotate the straw as you dip.

Instructions

1. Dip the straw in the solution, as you did with the Bubble Burst.

2. Blow into the straw very, very gently. There's a threshhold of breath pressure—which you can only find by practicing—between either blowing a *lot* of bubbles or *one*.

Blow gently, and your bubble will keep growing.

3. When you're ready to separate the bubble from the straw, either blow harder or simply flick the straw—the bubble will slide off the end of it.

THE EXPANDING BUBBLE

Professor's Notes

Now you're going to use your straw to make a bubble grow. This simple trick amazes people almost as much as any other.

Why? Because most of us think of bubbles as fragile objects that can't be changed. Yet here, with just a straw, you'll make a bubble bigger or smaller whenever you want.

Level: Intermediate, because you've got to learn two beginner's tricks to do it.

Science: Here's proof that dryness pops bubbles: You can insert the straw into a bubble only if it's wet. Make a comparison. Try it with a dry straw, and see what happens.

Instructions

1. Blow a bubble, catch it on the end of a bubble wand.

Start off with a small bubble. The smaller the bubble you start with, the more amazing it is.

2. Dip the straw into the solution.

3. Gently insert the straw into the wall of the bubble.

4. Suck inward gently, to break the bubble film at the end of the straw.

5. Gently exhale, and continue blowing, getting your warm breath inside the bubble. Gradually, the bubble will expand until it pops.

THE BUBBLE TAIL

As you work with the bubble and straw, you'll notice something that you may have overlooked before—the bubble's "tail."

What's a Bubble Tail?

Bubbles are affected by gravity; it keeps pulling bubble solution from the top of the bubble down to the bottom of the bubble.

As the solution is pulled to the bottom, it forms little drops. These drops are what I call "tails."

If you're making big bubbles, or if you're just blowing bubbles into the air, these tails won't make much difference. But when you work with more than one bubble at a time—or with bubbles and bubble film (as you'll

be doing in the next chapter), the tails become your enemy.

The reason: Those wet drops of bubble solution break the surface tension on other bubbles, causing the two bubbles (or bubble and bubble film) to join.

How to Get Rid of the Tail

•Hold the bubble on a wand in one hand, and a wet straw in the other.
•Use the straw to wipe off the little drop of solution (the tail) at the bottom of the bubble.
•Shake all the extra solution off the straw.

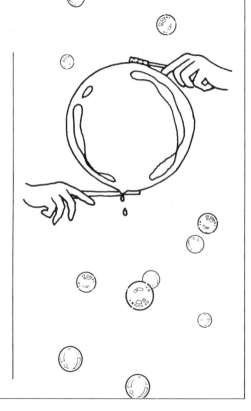

A BUBBLE IN A BUBBLE

Professor's Notes

This is the simplest way to blow a bubble inside a bubble; it's much easier than the method explained in the previous chapter.

Level: Intermediate.

Tips: Patience, patience. This is technically easy, but can still be frustrating because the wet bubbles often join on the bottom and become one big bubble.

•Do not inhale, the way you did with the exanding bubble.

•Insert your straw from the top, so it enters the bubble at a 45-degree angle. Typically, beginners put the straw in at a bad angle, and the inside bubble creeps up the straw and joins the outside bubble.

Instructions

1. Blow a Basic Bubble and catch it on the wand.

2. Dip the straw in the solution and get it wet. Then insert the straw through the side of the bubble on the bubble wand.

TIPS

- The first bubble doesn't have to be big—because as you're blowing a bubble inside it, the original bubble will expand.
- If the inside bubble hangs off the end of the straw instead of popping off, give it an extra puff or a flip of the wrist, and it will slip off.
- If you blow too hard, you'll get a lot of little bubbles inside the bubble (instead of one big one). So remember to exhale very gently through the straw.

3. Blow gently, and make one big bubble on the end of the straw.
Hint: Before inserting the straw into the Basic Bubble, you should blow a 2-inch Glassblower's Bubble—it uses up the excess solution.

Mr. Bubbles' Tips:
As the inside bubble comes off the straw, blow a little puff of air into the bigger bubble. It'll make the inside bubble spin around.

THE BUBBLE FRAME

Bubble Wave • Wall of Bubbles • Bubble Trampoline • Giant Bubbles • Bubble Twist

So far we've only worked with small bubbles—4 to 6 inches—because that's the biggest we could make with the tools we had. But...with a bigger wand, we can make bigger bubbles.

In this chapter, we'll make our first oversize wand using simple materials. I call it a "bubble frame."

The "bubble frame" is one of the most versatile tools in bubble-ology. It's simple, flexible, and fascinating. You can use it to perform tricks, experiment with bubble science, play games, and best of all, make enormous bubbles. People will be astounded.

PREPARATION

Materials You Need:

•Cotton string—the kind you can get at a grocery or hardware store. (I don't like to use nylon string—it doesn't seem absorbent enough.)

•Ordinary plastic drinking straws.

•A bowl to pour the bubble solution into. I usually use a shallow cake dish about 8-10 inches in diameter, but there are lots of other good bowls to work with, too: You can use a big plastic cereal bowl about the size of a saucer, an aluminum pie tin, or a foil baking dish.

Note: The whole straw has to be able to fit into the bowl. If you can't get a big enough bowl, cut off the straws until they fit into the one you've got.

Set-Up:

•Roll up your sleeves and plan to get your hands wet at least up to your wrists.

•Indoors, you might get the floors wet, due to dripping and popping of huge bubbles. Put newspapers on the floor—about 6 of them, spread out, with your bowl of bubble solution in the center.

TIPS

Aluminum dishes are particularly good to use with the bubble frame because they're deep enough for the bubble solution, and wide enough for the straws. Plus, when you're done, you can bend the corner into little spout and pour the solution back into the bottle. I recommend:

•The EZ Foil Casserole and Lasagna Pan—bought in a hardware store, 2 for $1.89. The size is 11 1/4" long, by 9 1/4" wide, by 1 3/4" deep.

BUBBLE BASICS

How to Make Your Bubble Frame

1. Take the cotton string. Cut off a piece about 5 feet long. [For younger bubble-ologists, 3 feet will work fine.]

2. Thread one end of the string through two straws.

Mr. Bubbles' Tips:
You may want to use a piece of wire to help push the string through the straw. But if the string and straw are both dry, it should be no problem.

3. Tie the ends of the string together in a simple knot. Cut off the extra. Now you've got a loop of string with two straws on it. Slide the knot inside one of the straws, to get it out of the way.

4. The straws are handles. Take one straw in each hand, and pull the string apart. You should now be holding a rectangle. Make sure everything's evenly spaced.

Now you've got a fantastic, simple bubble hoop, which we can use to make gigantic soap bubbles.

BUBBLE BASICS

To Make the Bubble Film:

1. Pour the bubble solution into your bowl.

2. Dip the bubble frame into the bowl. Everything goes in—straws, string, *and* your hands (or at least your fingers).This is important; if you don't get your hands wet, their dryness will pop the bubbles.

3. Gently lift the frame out of the bubble solution. You can hold one straw in each hand, or hold the two straws together in one hand. Try them both, and use the method that works best for you. Do not open the frame until the next step.

4. Slowly pull the straws apart, until the string is tight. If you're careful, you'll get a bubble film that fills up the frame.

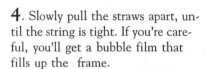

Mr. Bubbles' Tips: Hold the straws tightly, but don't pull on them, because they'll bend. To keep the frame stiff, just keep your hands straight.

If Your Bubble Film Keeps Popping:

• Your straws and string might not be completely wet.

• Your hands might be too dry.

• If you're outside, the wind might be blowing it out. Solution: Hold your frame so the wind blows *across*, not *into* the film as you open it.

• In the winter time (or any time when the air is very dry), the bubbles tend to evaporate very quickly. So you may need to add a bit of glycerine or dishwashing detergent to your solution to thicken it...or just mix up some Bubble Solution #2.

SCIENCE

To see how light reflects off bubbles, pretend the bubble film is a mirror.

Hold it so you get a reflection from a white ceiling, and you will see a lot of color. But if you turn it towards a dark wall, you lose the color... because there's little light being reflected.

Outside, notice how trees and the sky are reflected in the bubble film.

THE BUBBLE WAVE

Professor's Notes

This is one of the most popular projects for beginners because it's very easy, but incredibly beautiful. Kids especially love it.

Level: Beginner.

Place: Indoors (or outside, if there's not much wind).

Tips: Work quickly. The longer you wait with bubble film, the harder it becomes to play with, because it starts to evaporate.
•For the prettiest effect, get as much light reflecting off your bubble wave as possible.

Science: This is how all waves move, whether they're light or ocean waves.

Instructions

1. Hold the frame in front of you.
•Keep your arms straight.
•Don't pull too hard on the frame.

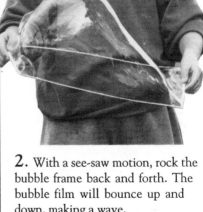

2. With a see-saw motion, rock the bubble frame back and forth. The bubble film will bounce up and down, making a wave.
•Keep it going until the waves get too high and hit a dry spot on your hand.

THE GIANT WAVE

The more people who use the bubble frame together, the more fun the tricks are—and the more impressive the results. But be ready—it's harder to make bubble tricks work when you have to pay careful attention to what other people are doing.

The wave is fun to do with a bunch of people—2, 3, 4...even 10! We'll demonstrate it here with 3.

Reminder: This is a team effort, so it may take a few tries to get it right. Keep working at it!

Getting Ready

•Cut a piece of cotton string 15 to 20 feet long. Tie the ends together. Now you have a giant loop of string.
•Use the same dish of bubble solution you've already been using.

Now:

1. Everybody picks up the string and steps back until it is stretched tight. Spread out so you're spaced evenly apart. The dish of bubble solution is on the ground, between all of you.

2. Everyone walks to the middle where the bowl is.

3. Dip the whole string in carefully, so it doesn't get tangled up. Everyone should keep holding onto it.

4. At the same time, everybody puts their hands into the dish. If the bowl isn't big enough, get the string wet first and then take turns getting your hands wet.

5. On the count of three, everyone raises their hands straight out of the bowl, almost touching one another.

6. Gently, everyone walks backwards and makes the string tight, the way it was at the start. As you do this, you get a gigantic bubble film.

7. Shake one or two sides of the loop gently, rocking it the way you rocked the Bubble Wave, and you'll get giant waves.

TIPS

If the film keeps popping, it might be because:
- There's too strong a wind.
- Someone hasn't gotten his or her hands wet enough.
- There's too much liquid on the frame. Excess bubble solution flows toward the middle of the frame, and its weight is sometimes so great that it pops the film. One way to avoid it: When you lift the string out of the bubble solution, hold it over the dish for a few seconds and let some of the bubble solution drip off.

Mr. Bubbles' Tips:

You can make a Giant Bubble Wave with just a 4-ounce jar of my Mr. Bubbles ™ solution!

THE WALL OF BUBBLES

Professor's Notes

In this trick, we use the Bubble Frame like a giant bubble wand, blowing a bubble out of the film.

Level: Beginner-plus.

Place: Anywhere there's room, indoors or out. Floor *will* get a little wet.

Tips: Make a smaller frame before you start, and experiment with both sizes. You'll find that you can have just as much fun with a small frame as a big one. In fact, I often *prefer* working with a small frame (like the one in the photos).

Instructions

1. Hold the bubble film in front of your face, about 8 to 10 inches away from it.

2. Blow gently, as if you were blowing a bubble with a bubble wand. Bubbles will come out of the wall. *How* you blow will affect your results:

• If you blow continuously, you'll blow a big bubble.

• If you blow short and sharp, you're creating a small blast of air that'll make small bubbles.

Use the Wind

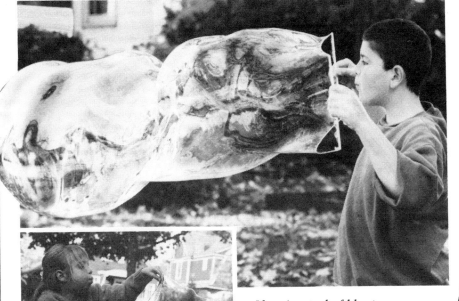

If you're tired of blowing, put your frame on auto-bubble. Hold it up to the wind, and you can get automatic bubbles.

TIPS:
- When you're blowing a bubble out of the middle of the frame, blow upward. If you blow down, the bubble will fall to the ground too quickly.
- If you blow too hard, you'll blow the film right off.
- Outdoors tip: The stronger the breeze, the harder it is to work with a big frame. So when there's a lot of wind, use a small one. Ideal size frame for a medium breeze: 5" X 7".
- Be patient. It will take a while to figure out how to get this right.

THE BUBBLE TRAMPOLINE

Professor's Notes

One day, while I was playing around with the bubble frame, I discovered that a little bubble would bounce off bubble film—just like a trampoline. And I found that if you raise the bubble frame to hit that little bubble, you can bounce it higher and higher— until it pops. It's a neat trick, but it can be frustrating at first. Keep at it.

Level: Intermediate.

Place: Indoors only.

Science: As we discussed earlier, "surface tension" in bubble walls generally prevents bubbles from joining each other. The same thing happens between a bubble and bubble *film*.

Instructions

1. Blow a 4-inch bubble out of the bubble wall, up into the air. Hold the frame out in front of you.
Hint: While the bubble is in the air, tilt the bubble frame and drain the excess water from it.

2. As the bubble falls, raise the trampoline gently to meet it. Hit the bottom of the bubble and bounce it up into the air.

Professor Bubbles' Challenge

• How many bubbles can you get going at once?

• How many times you can make a bubble bounce on the trampoline?

• How good is your teamwork? This is a 2-person challenge. One of you blows bubbles with a bubble wand, while the other tries to bounce them off the trampoline.

The Swimming Bubble

A bubble doesn't always bounce off the trampoline—sometimes it gets caught in the frame instead. When this happens, you have a whole different kind of fun. The bubble slides around inside the frame like it's swimming.

Can you teach your bubble to do the backstroke?

By the way—some people call this the Fried Egg Bubble (it looks like a fried egg) and some call it the Flying Saucer Bubble. What do you think?

Hints:

• If the bubble you blow is too big or if you get a bunch of bubbles, the trampoline probably won't work—so start again.

TIPS

• If there's a little tail on the bottom of the bubble (see p. 29) when it lands on the trampoline, it will break the surface tension of the bubble film, and the two will join.

• If the bubble solution on the film is very thick and wet, the bubble will join instead of bouncing. To avoid this, tilt the bubble trampoline slightly so the excess moisture runs off the edge.

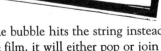

• If the bubble hits the string instead of the film, it will either pop or join into the bubble film.

GIANT BUBBLES

Professor's Notes

Big bubbles like these are my favorites. They're spectacularly beautiful to look at, and I love watching them float up into the air, taking on all different sizes and shapes as they struggle to become round. You're going to enjoy this!

Level: Intermediate

Place: Outside (or indoors, if you've got some ceiling room). When they pop, they're very wet.

Instructions

1. Hold the bubble frame in front of you, parallel to the ground. Your arms should be fairly stiff.

2. Raise the bubble frame toward the sky, gently swinging out your arms and filling the bubble film full of air. You will actually get a tube of bubble film.

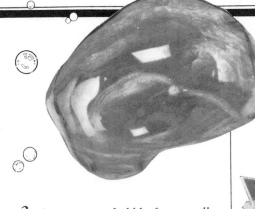

3. As a gigantic bubble forms, pull the frame away from the bubble and towards you. Give it a little downward twist to close off the end of the bubble.

4. The bubble will automatically float out in front of you, and up into the air.

HINT: If you have trouble removing the frame, step backwards as you make the bubble.

TIPS

- It's much easier to make smaller bubbles, so you might want to try making 8- or 12-inch bubbles at first, and keep practicing until you get good at it.
- To make smaller bubbles, just move the frame a little more gently.
- As you get better at that, you can start putting more and more air inside the bubbles, making the tube longer and longer before you close it off. Keep doing this until you get the feel of it.

Now we get to the *really* big stuff! You can make a bigger loop—as you did with the Bubble Wave—and make a huge bubble with 2, 3, 4 or more people.

To get a feel for it, start with a 2-person bubble. Make your film, and then move the frame upward together, watching the enormous tube of bubble film form. Then try moving the frame sideways...and then try running into the wind.

THE BUBBLE TWIST

Professor's Notes

Because the bubble frame is flexible, you can bend it over—and turn it into a double-bubble wand!

Level: Advanced.

Place: Indoors with smaller frame. Outside is best.

Science: Watch what happens to the bubble film as you flip one straw over. You'll discover that you can actually make the bubble film curve!

Tips: For double-bubbles, you can use a slighty larger bubble frame. Try using about 8 feet of string.

Instructions

1. Take the bubble frame and twist it so that the string makes a big X, forming two triangles. Dip it into the bubble solution.

Alternative method: Dip the frame into the bubble solution first, and *then* twist it over into an X.

2. Now, use the same motion you did with the giant bubble—and you will launch two bubbles at the same time.

Alternative method: If you prefer, you can blow two bubbles out with your breath.

ADVANCED BUBBLE-OLOGY

This is an excercise for experts. We'll combine three of the tricks in this chapter—the Bubble Wall, the Bubble Trampoline, and the Giant Bubble—to make one spectacular one.

We'll bounce a bubble on the trampoline, and then as it closes up, we'll quickly put it inside another, bigger bubble.

Reminder: The longer bubbles and bubble films are in existence, the thinner they become—and the harder they are to work with. So while doing complicated tricks, work as quickly and efficiently as possible.

Instructions

1. Make a bubble trampoline and a bubble to bounce on it.

2. Bounce it once. Let the bubble wave sink. As the wave goes down, raise the handles of the bubble frame and make a giant bubble around the little bubble.

Voila! You're a bubble magician!

"A soap bubble is the most beautiful thing, and the most exquisite in nature...I wonder how much it would take to buy a soap bubble if there was only one in the world?"

—Mark Twain,
The Innocents Abroad

HAND-MADE BUBBLES

Two-handed Bubble • Barehanded Bubble • Double Bubble • Dancing Bubble •Bubble Chain

Most people would never suspect it, but the simplest, most versatile bubble-making tools available are the ones you're born with—your hands.

They're very practical.

Besides being easy to use (you've been practicing all your life), they're efficient, cheap...and you've always got a pair along with you.

Of course, they're also messy...but that's part of the fun. So in this chapter, we'll put all our other tools aside and just make bubbles with our bare hands.

Holding a bubble in your hands is a wonderful feeling.

PREPARATION

Materials You'll Need

- A dish or bowl (or aluminum pan).
- Mr. Bubbles ™ bubble solution.
- Paper towels to wipe your hands with.
- Additives for Bubble Solution #2 (glyycerine, Dawn detergent, water).
- Newspaper (to put on the floor if you do this indoors).
- You *can* use straight bubble solution, but if the bubbles pop too easily, you should mix up a batch of Bubble Solution #2 and use that instead.
- This is especially true if you're making bubbles in the winter time, when the humidity is dry.

Set-Up

- You're going to get wet doing this. It's soapy, slippery, foamy, and in-credi-bubble fun!
- It's really an outside activity (although it's also possible to practice while washing dishes or in the bathtub). If you do it inside, cover the floor with newspaper.

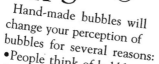

TIPS

Hand-made bubbles will change your perception of bubbles for several reasons:

- People think of bubbles as fragile—and they are—but here you're actually able to grab them and play with them.
- You get to experience the bubble through a sense of touch, which not only adds a dimension of understanding, but feels good, too.

- Don't do it on grass— it'll turn the grass brown.
- It doesn't hurt to be within reasonable distance of a hose for clean-up. (To get rid of suds, use a fine spray.)

BUBBLE BASICS

I first learned about hand-made bubbles from a California bubble-ologist named Sterling Johnson. He showed me how to dip my hands into bubble solution and form a bubble film between them.

Now it's your turn. Here's the Basic Position for blowing two-handed bubbles.

Getting Ready

1. Pour the bubble solution into your bowl (or aluminum pan).

2. Dip your hands in. Get both of them completely wet with solution — front and back—up to your wrist.

The Basic Position

Now you're going to make an opening, like a bubble wand, between your thumbs and index fingers. Think of it as a "bubble window."

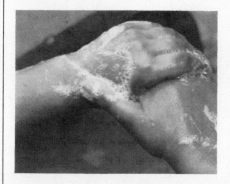

Instructions

1. With the backs of your hands toward you, put one hand on top of the other. Lay your fingers across the knuckles of the bottom hand. Tuck thumb under hand.

2. Slide your hands slowly apart, forming a bubble film between your thumbs and index fingers.

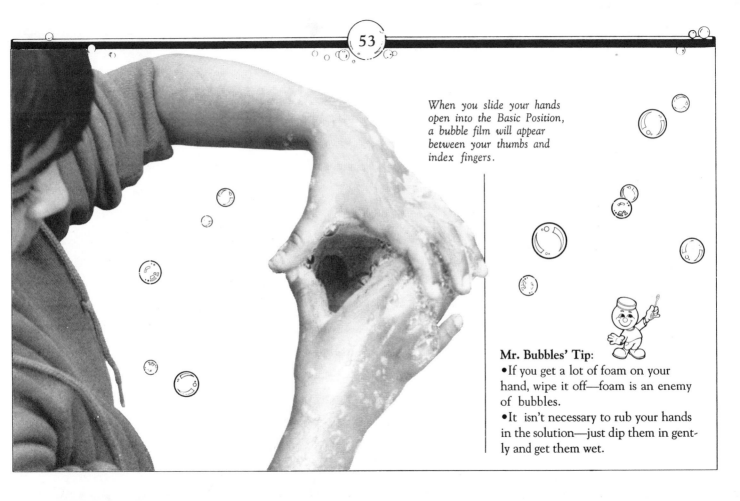

When you slide your hands open into the Basic Position, a bubble film will appear between your thumbs and index fingers.

Mr. Bubbles' Tip:
• If you get a lot of foam on your hand, wipe it off—foam is an enemy of bubbles.
• It isn't necessary to rub your hands in the solution—just dip them in gently and get them wet.

TWO-HANDED BUBBLES

Professor's Notes

Some people are reluctant to try this at first, because they "don't want to get wet."

Then, while they're doing tricks with bubbles, they get a little foam on their hands, and say, "Well, I'm already a little wet...."

So they start blowing bubbles with their hands. All of a sudden, they're having a ball...because this is one of the most enjoyable things you can do with bubbles. Especially in summer.

Level: Intermediate.

Place: Outdoors.

Tips: Don't worry about the mess...just have fun!

Instructions

1. Dip your hands in the bubble solution, getting them completely wet.

2. Form a bubble film across them, and hold them about 8 to 10 inches from your face.

3. Blow on the bubble film as if you were making a Basic Bubble.

•Practice your breath control to see

how hard to blow. I generally tell people to blow gently, but it really depends on your lung capacity. Younger kids, for example, may have to blow harder.

•When you get the right breath velocity, a bubble will start coming out of your hands.

•If you blow gently enough, the bubble will *continue* to come out of your hands. It doesn't just pop out, the way it does on a wand.

4. Finishing the bubble is the hardest part. To close it off, you can either blow hard enough so the bubble pops off naturally, or—if you're blowing a larger bubble—you can close your hands around the bubble (bring them together palm to palm, like clapping or praying) as it gets bigger and bigger.

• With a little practice, you can make bubbles that are a foot in diameter...or more!

Mr. Bubbles' Tips:

One way to control bubbles is to adjust the distance you hold your hands from your mouth. The farther away you hold them, the gentler your breath is on the film.

•If you're having trouble blowing big bubbles—or any bubbles, for that matter—you probably don't have enough solution on your hands. Make sure your hands are wet on both the front and the back.

•After you've had your hands out of the bubble solution for about 30 seconds, the solution evaporates and your hands get dry again. So you have to re-wet them.

•Tilt your hands up a little bit when you make bubbles, so you're blowing up instead of down. That's how you get the bubble off your hands.

BUBBLE SPRAY

Professor's Notes

In this trick, you use your hands to blow a bunch of little bubbles instead of one big one.

Kids love this—in fact, I learned it by watching a little girl in my neighborhood. She was playing with bubbles and had lots of suds on her hands. So she blew on her hands to get the foam off—and bubbles came out instead.

Level: Beginner.

Place: Outdoors.

Tips: Blow a little harder on your hands than before, because now the openings are pretty small.

•Blow up and down, over your whole hand, to get all the bubbles out.

Instructions

1. Get your hands soaking wet again.

2. Interlock your fingers, as if praying.

3. Slide them apart, until all of the tips of your fingers are touching each other.

•You are creating 6 openings—6 little bubble wands—in your hands.

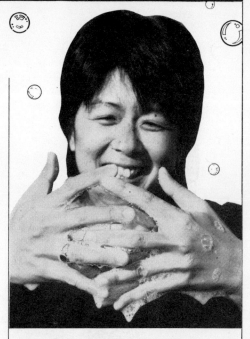

4. Hold your hands 8 to 10 inches away from your face, and blow.
•Hold your hands far enough away so that you can blow hard on them.

TIPS

Bubble Harvest

The whole idea behind this trick is to create six bubble openings by *touching* your fingers together.

- If your fingers aren't touching, then you're not completing the bubble wands.
- That will still work—but you get the *most* bubbles if all your fingers are together.

BAREHANDED BUBBLES

Now you're ready to pluck a bubble out of the air and hold it. Because your hands are wet, the bubble will just stay there—it won't pop.

Instructions

1. First, get your whole arm wet up to the elbow. The bubble will pop if it touches your dry wrist.

2. Blow a bubble and catch it on the flat part of your hand.

•Your hand is such a large surface that if you hold it flat, the bubble will stick to it.

•Experiment. Hold it upside down, wave it around...see what happens.

Mr. Bubbles' Tips:

Try putting a straw inside of it—blow a bubble inside of a bubble!

Getting Inside a Bubble

One of the most amazing things you can do at this stage, is actually put your finger...or your hand...or your whole arm...right into a bubble.

The bubble won't pop as long as your hand is completely wet...and is free from suds.

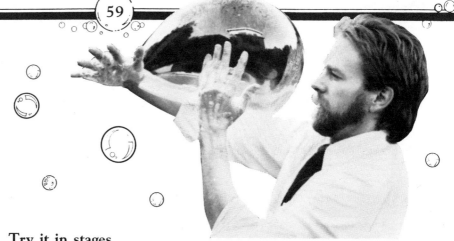

Try it in stages

• Hold a bubble in one hand. Put a finger from the other hand right into the top of the bubble (it's easier from the top).

• Now try it with your open hand. Make sure it's wet all the way up to the wrist. You'll find it's a weird sensation—kind of a ticklish feeling—as the bubble film slides up your fingers and up the back of your hand.

• Angle your hand down a little bit so the bubble film doesn't slide onto your wrist.

• And finally, try putting your whole arm in. You need a very big bubble for this, so you may have to use the Bubble Frame to make it instead of your hands. When you're inserting your whole arm, move slowly and gently or you'll pop the bubble.

THE BUBBLE CYLINDER

Professor's Notes

If you hold the bubble with both your wet hands, you can stretch it out into a cylinder and hold it in that shape for a little while.

Level: Beginner.

Place: Outdoors—or indoors if you don't mind getting the floor a little wet.

Science: As you stretch the bubble, you'll find that the surface tension forces the bubble to break into two— and you suddenly have one bubble on each hand.

Tips: Keep your hands as flat as possible so the bubble has a large surface to stick to.

How long does one last?

The farther you stretch the bubble, the quicker it disappears.
An 8 to 10 inch cylinder might last as long as a few minutes.

How Far Can You Stretch?

I've made bubble cylinders about 2 1/2 feet long—how long can you make them?

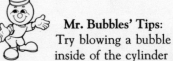

Mr. Bubbles' Tips:
Try blowing a bubble inside of the cylinder while you're holding it.. Turn it over and let it fall down to the other side.

THE DANCING BUBBLE

Shake It Up Baby

Here's another way to handle a bubble: Make it dance. Shake it up and down, sideways...whatever works for you. Do it to music.

They're naturally beautiful and colorful.

As bubbles vibrate, they reflect color from every direction.

Slow Dancing

You can make it undulate by moving very slowly. I call this the Arabian Dancing Bubble.

Fast Dancing

Make it wiggle and jiggle to rock 'n' roll. You get vibrations all over the bubble, and it begins to resemble an alien creature from a low-budget science fiction movie.

Bigger Is Better

The bigger the bubble, the more fantastic the effect of shaking it is. You *can* shake a bubble that's only 6 inches wide, but the effect is much more impresive when you do it with a bubble that's 1 foot in diameter. That's the size I enjoy most.

ONE-HANDED BUBBLES

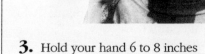

Professor's Notes

Now that you've made bubbles with both hands at once, you're ready to try making them one-handed.

Level: Intermediate.

Place: Again, it's an outdoors activity that you can do indoors if the floor is protected.

Tips: Your hands must be completely wet.

•When you put your fingers together to make a loop, they must be touching each other.

1. Dip your hand in the bubble solution. Put your thumb flat against your forefinger as you take it out of the pan.

2. Make an "OK" sign by touching the tip of your thumb to the tip of your first finger. A bubble film should form across the "O."

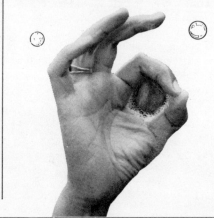

3. Hold your hand 6 to 8 inches away from your face.
•**The best way to position your hand**: With your palm facing down and your fingers spread out.

4. Blow gently on the film and begin making a bubble.

Note: You *can* blow a bubble with your palm facing up, but it's harder because the weight of the bubble will often pull it down and pop it on your wrist.

4. When you see a bubble forming, stop and gently close your thumb toward your forefinger, leaving a bubble on your hand.
• If your palm is facing down, the

bubble is hanging off your palm.

5. To release it:
•The bubble is on your hand; your palm is downward.
•Let the excess water drain off it.
•Gently throw the bubble up and withdraw your hand, and it comes right off the end.

Method #2: The Biggest Handmade Bubble
Here's an alternative way to blow a bubble through one hand (although you need both hands to do it). It's also the way you make the biggest possible bubble with your hands.

1. Blow a bubble through one hand directly onto the palm of the other hand (palm must be wet).
•Keep pulling your palm away as you blow the bubble, to give it room to expand.

•The less area a bubble is touching, the easier it is to get it off your hand.

•When your bubble is as big as you want it, close your hand into a fist and let the bubble hang down from it.

2. The bubble will look like a cylinder while it's being blown. But when you stop blowing (and stretching it out), it's round.

TWIN BUBBLES #2

You've got two hands....

… So make a one-handed bubble in each of them.
•Remember that when you're making two bubbles at once, you want to work fast, so the bubbles don't evaporate.

When you're holding two bubbles, you can hold them with your palms up…or palms down.

It's like holding a crystal ball in each of your hands.

It's a strange feeling to hold two bubbles in your hands.

Science Note : Bring the two bubbles in your hands toward each other. Push them together, and you'll see that they won't join due to surface tension.

Mr. Bubbles' Tips:
There's another, easier way to get two bubbles at once. Here's how: Hold an 8-inch bubble in one of your wet hands. Close the other hand over the end of the bubble, like a claw, and gently pull it apart. You'll actually pull out another bubble.

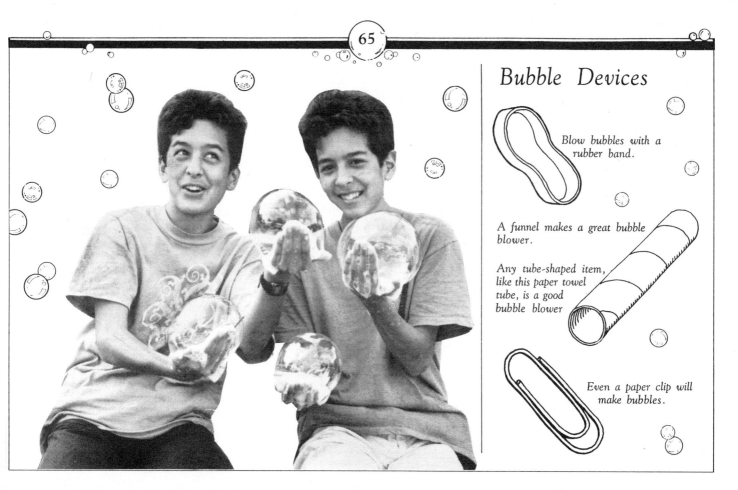

Bubble Devices

Blow bubbles with a rubber band.

A funnel makes a great bubble blower.

Any tube-shaped item, like this paper towel tube, is a good bubble blower

Even a paper clip will make bubbles.

DOUBLE BUBBLE #2

Professor's Notes

This Double Bubble is essentially the same trick you did earlier with bubble wands. But here we're no longer limited by the size of the wand. Now we can work with bubbles that are a foot in diameter…or larger….And these bubbles are more fragile and more beautiful.

Level: Intermediate.

Science: If the bubbles are the same size, the area where they join is actually flat because the air pressure inside them is equal.

•If one bubble is smaller, the wall between the two bubbles is curved into the *larger* of the two bubbles. The reason: Air pressure is greater in small bubbles than in large ones.

1. With your bubble wand, your hands, or any tool you want to use, blow a bubble and catch it with a wet hand.

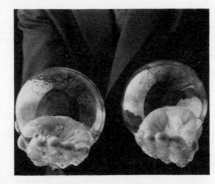

2. Blow a second bubble in your other wet hand, using the one-handed bubble technique. Now you've got a bubble in each hand.

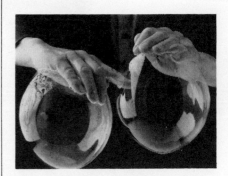

3. Bring the bubbles together gently. As you do, insert a wet finger into the wall of one of them. This breaks the surface tension.

4. The bubbles magically join.

For two people: Try to join your bubble to someone else's bubble.

TIPS

- It's easier to join bubbles when they're hanging down from your palms.
- After you learn to put bubbles together, you'll find that you can pull them apart, too. You can keep doing it until, at some point, they join together and make one big bubble.

THE BUBBLE CHAIN

Professor's Notes

In this trick, we use the one-handed-technique to build a chain of bubbles, attaching them together as we blow them. So this bubble formation actually *grows*!

With practice, you can make a chain of 5 or more bubbles.

Level: Advanced

Tips: A chain is easier to make if you blow each succeeding bubble a little smaller than the last one.

•Until you get the feel of this trick, you might want to practice it in front of a mirror and watch your hands.

•You'll *have* to practice—it's hard!

Learn to Move Fast

The longer bubbles last, the more fragile they become, because bubble solution evaporates.

•Most beginners move slowly, so by the time they get to the third bubble in the chain, the first one has disappeared.

•This can be frustrating at first. But once you get the feel of it, you move very quickly. For example, I can make a chain of 5 to 6 bubbles in about 10 seconds.

•So remember you're shooting for speed, which takes the coordination of blowing, closing off, blowing, closing off—and lots of breath control.

Blow through the "O," onto the palm of your other hand.

Instructions

The basis of the bubble chain is Method #2 of the One-handed Bubble.

1. Wet your hands. Blow a bubble through one hand onto the palm of the other hand.

2. Close off the "O" and seal off the bubble.

3. Open the "O" again, and you have a new bubble film.

4. Blow a new bubble onto the surface of the first one. The new bubble will be attached to the first one. Close it off again.

5. Keep repeating this.
•The trick is to keep moving your hands apart, to make room for the new bubble.

Seal off the bubble by closing the "O."

Blow a new bubble onto the first one.

TIPS

•After you've made three bubbles, you'll probably have tails on them, which make the chain too heavy to hold together as its length increases.

•To get rid of the tails: Hold the chain vertically, and let all the water drain off into your hands.

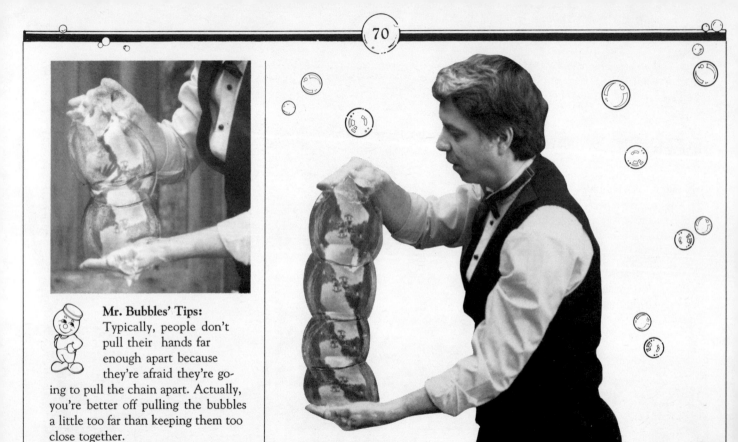

Mr. Bubbles' Tips:
Typically, people don't pull their hands far enough apart because they're afraid they're going to pull the chain apart. Actually, you're better off pulling the bubbles a little too far than keeping them too close together.

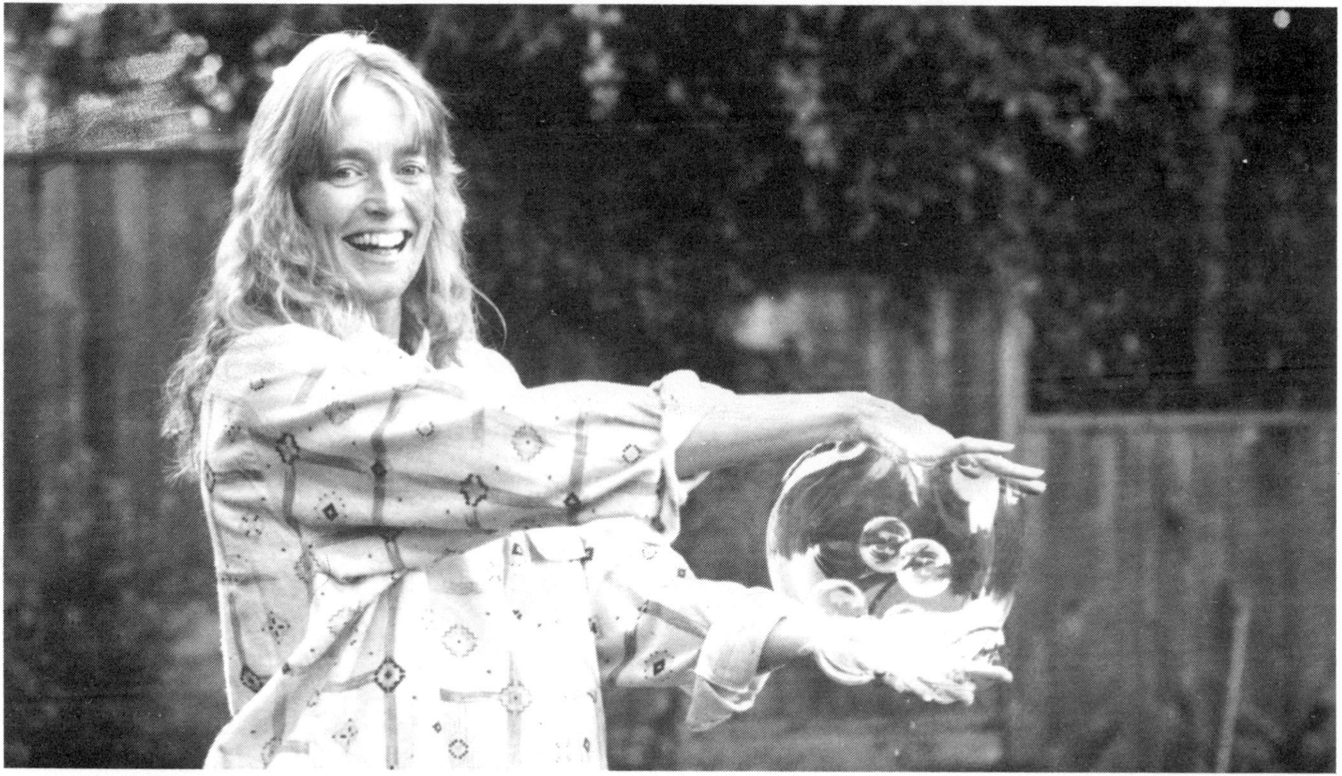

COATHANGER HOOPS

Giant Bubbles • Doughnut Bubbles • Rainbow Bubbles • Bubble Tubes • Bubble Sculpture

We made giant bubbles with the Bubble Frame in Chapter Three. Now, in this chapter, I'm going to show you how to make the same kind of spectacular bubbles—and more—with homemade hoops.

Constructing your own hoops is an interesting skill to learn, and coathanger hoops are perfect for beginners. They're inexpensive, fun to make, and amazingly easy to use....So easy, in fact, that you'll look like an expert the first time you use one.

Now let's begin some new experiments in bubble-ology.

You're never too old to have fun with bubbles.

PREPARATION

Materials You'll Need

•A wire coat hanger (Any kind will work, but I find that thin ones are easier to bend).

•String (the same cotton twine you used in your Bubble Frame), and scissors to cut it with.

•A pair of pliers.

•A tray for your bubble solution—a disposable foil tray, a frying pan, a cookie tray, or anything that the hoop fits into.

•Bubble solution. For the tricks in this chapter, we need to make up a batch of Solution #2 (including glycerine, Dawn, Mr. Bubbles ™, bubble solution).

Making Bubbles Outdoors

•One of the things we learn with bubbles is to be aware of the weather and how it's affecting us. Different kinds of days provide different kinds of fun.

•On a still day, because there's no air turbulence, you can make huge bubbles—4 to 5 feet in diameter.

•If there's a breeze, it's harder to make big bubbles because the wind pops them. But you *can* hold the hoop up to the breeze and twist it back and forth like a weather vane. The wind will blow out batches of bubbles.

•When there's a gentle breeze, you can blow really long tubes of bubbles.

•My favorite time to make bubbles is right after sunset or on a hazy day.

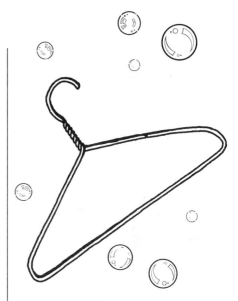

Mr. Bubbles' Tips:
This is easier to do in shade than in the bright sun because the sun beating down makes the bubble fluid evaporate.

BUBBLE BASICS

Cheap But Good

When I first started blowing bubbles in my backyard, kids from all over the neighborhood came over to play, but I didn't have enough bubble wands for everyone. So I created this cheap, easy-to-make hoop for them to use.

Note to Parents

A child may not be able to make this hoop unassisted. It requires enough dexterity and strength to be able to use a pair of pliers—so you may want to supervise (or help out with) this operation.

How to Make Your Hoop

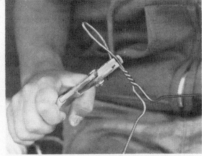

1. Take the pliers and bend the hooked end of the coathanger so it's flat.
• This is going to be the handle of the hoop.
• Be careful not to injure yourself when you're bending the hook.

2. Hold onto the top of the hanger (the handle), and pull the bottom (the long end) out, making the hanger into a square.
• If you want, you can stop right here and you've got a perfectly fine bubble maker.

BUBBLE BASICS

3. If you want to make your hoop round, bend the sides all the way around and form it into a circle (or as close as you can get).

Note: With the hoop as it is right now, you can make fairly large bubbles.
•But you can't make *huge* bubbles.
•The reason: Huge bubbles need *a*

lot of solution, and bare wire just can't hold enough.
•So we need to wrap string around the hoop. String is absorbent, adds more surface to the hoop, and creates pockets which hold extra solution. So...

4. Cut off a length of cotton string about 3 feet long.

5. Tie one end of the string onto the handle, and begin wrapping it around the hoop. It doesn't have to be tight, but don't leave it hanging too loose, either.

6. When you get back to the handle, you're still not done.
•Keep wrapping all the way up and down the handle until you run out of string.

•Or if you want, you can just wrap the handle separately.

It's important that the handle get wrapped well, because the wire will get too slippery by itself; string makes the handle easy to hold on to.
•Cover any exposed sharp metal parts with string.
•Cut off any excess string.

BUBBLE BASICS

Mr. Bubbles' Tips:
Make sure your hoop is as flat as possible. Take the time to bend it flat. And while you're at it, try bending the handle up, so it's easier to put the hoop in and out of the solution.

The Y Spot
The place most people miss when they're wrapping the coathanger is the "Y" at the base of the handle. Be sure to fill in that "Y" so there isn't any exposed wire there.
Easiest way: Just cross over with the string when you get all the way around, before you begin wrapping the handle.

Double String
If you aren't getting spectacular bubbles with your hoop, try wrapping a second length of string around the hoop, going in the opposite direction (sort of making X's with the string).
•Then you'll have more surface area and more pockets to hold bubble solution. Your bubbles will be bigger and sturdier.

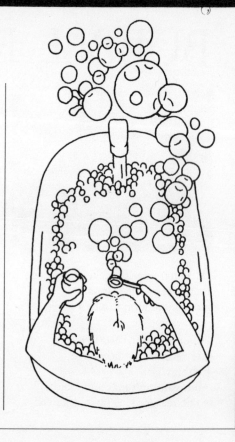

BUBBLE BASICS

Let's start with some "hoop technique."

Dipping Your Hoop
Beginners usually slosh their hoops around in the bubble solution to get them wet. That just creates foam, and it's unnecessary.

Correct Way: Place the hoop in the solution and leave it there for a few seconds until it's soaked through. If you need to, force the hoop down gently into the solution with one hand.

Lifting Your Hoop Out of the Pan
It's important to get as few little sudsy bubbles in your solution as possible, so don't raise the hoop straight up out of the bubble solution. That creates little bubbles in the pan (and breaks the film on the hoop).

Correct Way: Turn the hoop on its side, perpendicular to the tray, while it's still in the solution.
•Gently lift it that way. You won't create foam, and you'll have a better, more reliable bubble film.

The Enemy
The more people there are playing with bubble solution at the same time, the faster it collects extra bubbles and foam…which are the enemies of big bubbles. So it's important to keep removing the stuff from the top of your pan.

Some Ways to Do This
•Bend over the bubble pan and blow the foam off.
•Use a thin piece of plywood or shirt cardboard—or anything like it—to scrape foam off the top of the solution.

Mr. Bubbles' Tips: When I haven't got anything else, I just use my arm to push the foam off the pan. It's a little messy, but it works!

GREAT SHAPES

It really doesn't matter what shape your bubble hoops are—the bubbles will always come out round. But sometimes you can have more fun by bending the hoops into different shapes.

Here are a few examples of what *we've* done, but use your imagination. The sky's the limit....

Mr. Bubbles' Tips: Play indoor bubble basketball. Make a bubble and try to get it through a bubble hoop without breaking. Use your breath.

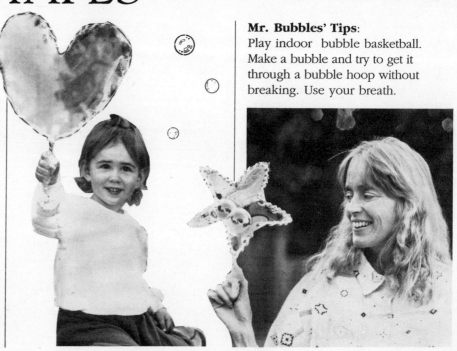

GIGANTIC BUBBLES

Professor's Notes

The first thing we'll do with the hoop is make enormous bubbles. By now you should be pretty comfortable with big bubbles— you've already made them with a Bubble Frame and with your hands. These are actually the easiest to do...so you can concentrate on experimenting.

Level: Intermediate

Place: Outdoors.

Tips: Start by making smaller bubbles with the hoop, and then work your way up to bigger ones.

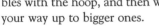

1. Dip your hoop into the solution and get a bubble film across it.

2. Wave your hoop into the air, making a tube. When the tube gets about three feet long, gently twist your wrist so you're twisting off the end of the bubble.

Important Note: Slow, gentle movements are best. Kids tend to swing hoops too fast, creating a huge rush of air which breaks the bubble film.

THE BUBBLE TUBE

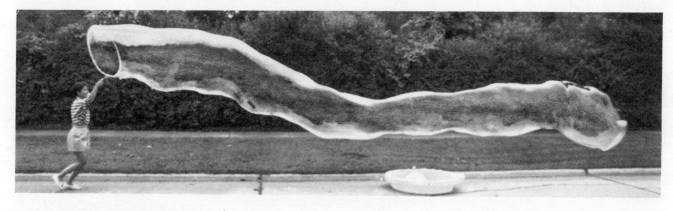

We're so used to thinking of bubbles as round that it's a surprise to see we can make them long, too.

A bubble tube is easy to make with these hoops. If there's even a slight breeze, you can create a tube from 3 to 10 feet long just by holding your hoop up and letting the wind blow it. I've made them 30 feet long!

If there isn't a breeze, you can wave the hoop in the air and make tubes...or you can run along, holding the hoop up over your shoulder, and make a bubble tube that follows you.

How long a tube can *you* make?

The life of a tube is really short—but there's something exciting about this fleeting natural phenomenon.

TUBULAR BUBBLES

Totally Tubular

It's a lot of fun to make bubble tubes in different shapes. Here are some you can try.

About the Weather

These bubbles never last long, and sometimes don't work at all. The biggest reason for that is weather.

•For example: If your solution is thick and the air is humid, the Doughnut Bubble is simple to do. But if the weather is dry or cold, or there's a heavy breeze, then it's a real struggle.

•So if you can't make these bubbles, it may not be your fault—more often than not, it's the weather conditions.

The Doughnut Bubble

A circular bubble that's connected all the way around, like a doughnut or a lifesaver.

Instructions

1. Hold the hoop about waist high; bring it straight up.

2. Curve it around and bring it back down in a sort of "U" shape (an upside-down U).

3. Make a second U-turn at your waist, and bring the hoop back to touch the beginning of the bubble.

Tip: Bring your hand straight up, and then around—by the time your hand gets to the bottom, the straight part will be curved.

The Doughnut Bubble

Around-the-World Bubble

A variation on the Doughnut Bubble.

•Make an 8-inch bubble, then do a doughnut around it. It lasts for only a few seconds, but is really exciting when you get it.

•It's a good 2-person bubble (one person makes the bubble, the other makes the doughnut).

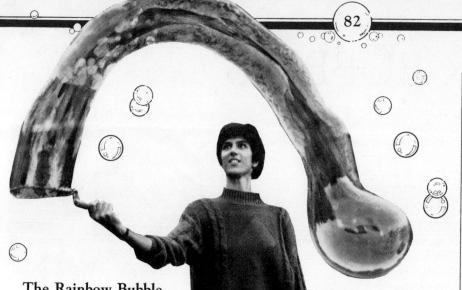

The Rainbow Bubble

Make a rainbow-shaped bubble over your head.

Instructions

1. Hold the hoop to one side of you, about at your knee.

2. Raise your arm in a gigantic arc, over your head.

3. Keep going, all the way down to your knee on the other side.

Tip: To get it to look like a rainbow, you have to start low—because by the time you get to the end, the first side of the bubble is rising.

The Lasso Bubble

Put a a bubble around your head; a variation of the Doughnut.

Instructions

1. Hold the hoop (with film on it) next to your head, but a little above it—so you're standing kind of like the Statue of Liberty.

2. Make a circular motion with your hand, around your head, creating a doughnut bubble over you. Alternative method: Spin around in place, with the same bubble results.

BUBBLE SCULPTURE

By dividing the opening of the hoop with string, you can create bubbles with many chambers and surfaces. They will take on all kinds of shapes as they float into the sky, and reflect light dramatically.

The artistry of this trick is in the designs you use to divide the bubble hoop. You can make any shapes and sizes on the frame—five openings, ten openings, a star, a square…use your imagination and experiment.

For our example, we picked a "quadri-bubble"—a bubble with four openings.

To Change Your Hoop

1. Tie a piece of cotton string to one side of the hoop. Stretch it across the opening and tie it onto the other side. Now you can make a bubble with two chambers.

2. If you divide that again, making an X across the hoop, you can make a bubble that's divided into four chambers.

See how easy it is? Now try it your way. What kind of crazy shapes can you make?

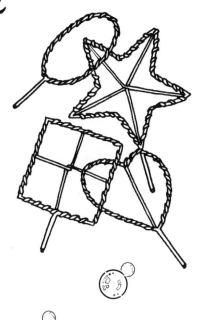

Make a bubble sculpture the same way you made giant bubbles.

Here's a demonstration of a quadri-bubble. It's easy…and beautiful.

BUBBLE TRICKS

Cable Car Bubble • Tightrope Bubble • Magic String • Body-Sized Bubbles • Giant Hoops

There are lots of simple bubble tricks that actually look like magic to people, because they're so unexpected. In this chapter, I'll teach you a few.

But this is just a sample of the surprising things that are possible with bubbles.

The fact is, bubble-ology is still so new that no one knows even a fraction of the things that can be done with the soapy spheres; people make important bubble discoveries all the time.

So after you learn these, be a pioneer; experiment with bubbles and invent your *own* tricks.

Proof that you can blow a bubble out of almost any opening: John Javna uses a lawn chair as a bubble wand. To try this, just spread bubble solution over the openings in the chair, hold it up, and blow. It's simple, and looks bizarre.

GIANT BUBBLE HOOPS

Now you can build your own gigantic bubble hoops.

The principle of the big bubble hoop is exactly the same as your coathanger hoop—except that the wire has to be thicker, it's harder to bend, and you need a larger pan. Plus, you need to mix up a lot more bubble solution.

Materials You'll Need

• 1/8-inch thick aluminum or steel wire. You can get it in 25- to 50-foot lengths at hardware stores.
• A pair of pliers.
• Cotton string—It should be thicker and heavier than the string you've been using for other chapters.

Instructions

1. Open up a length of wire and form it into a 3-foot diameter circle.

2. On each end, bend up about 9 inches of wire with a pair of pliers—that's the handle.

3. With string, lash these two halves of the handle together and wrap them the same way you did the handle of the coathanger hoop. Then tie them off.

4. 2 inches up the handle, bend it back almost 90 degrees. Now the handle looks a little like a frying pan handle—which makes it easier to dip in the solution.

5. Wrap the hoop the same way you wrapped the coathanger—going back and forth about four times. The more you wrap the hoop, the bigger and better the bubbles.

And that's it.

MAGIC STRING

You can blow a zillion small bubbles out of a loop of string. It takes no effort, and literally fills the air with 1-inch spheres. It's a great illusion—people wonder where all those bubbles are coming from!

Materials You'll Need
• A 3-foot piece of string.
• A dish, bowl, or pan.
• Mr. Bubbles ™ bubble solution.

Instructions

1. Tie the string into a loop.

2. Put your two index fingers into the loop and stretch it out.
•Now you have a loop of string that's an index finger wide, by 1 1/2 feet long.

3. Close your thumb and forefinger, holding the string tightly between them.

4. Lower the loop *and* the tips of your fingers into the bubble solution. Get your fingers wet!
•Don't swish it around—just get it wet.

5. Slowly lift the string out of the bubble solution, up to face level, about 10 inches away from your face.

6. Carefully stretch the string out again, so it's tight between your index fingers. You should now have a loop of string with a long, narrow bubble film.

7. Hold it about 8 inches away from your face, blow continuously from one side of the film to the other (from one finger to the other) back and forth, back and forth, and you'll blow a seemingly endless stream of bubbles.

TIGHTROPE BUBBLE

One day when I was working with Bubble Frames, I made a big bubble and accidentally caught it on the edge of the wet string. It just sat there. I thought, "Hey, if it'll sit there, it'll probably roll on the string, too." And it did.

That's how the trick was born.

Materials You'll Need
- A 4-foot piece of string.
- Bubble solution.
- A dish, bowl, or pan.

Tips: You must be working in a breeze-free environment.

- This bubble needs to be at least ten inches in diameter. If it's any smaller, it won't have enough weight to roll down the string.

- Keep practicing. This can be a hard one to learn.

Instructions

1. Make the string into a loop.

2. Loop your index and middle fingers over each end of the string.

3. Dip it all—including your hands—into the bubble solution. Get everything wet, then lift it out.

4. Pinch the loop to make it like a small bubble frame, and make (or blow) a bubble that's a foot in diameter.

- Easier method: Have someone else blow the bubble.

5. Quickly, while the bubble is floating in the air, blow hard on the string and get rid of the bubble film.
•The bubble film *must* be eliminated, or this trick won't work— the bubble will attach itself to the film instead of the string.

6. Quickly stretch out your hands so the loop is tight.

7. Reach over and catch the bubble on the string. The bubble will stick to it immediately.

8. Tilt your hands so the string is at a 45-degree angle, and gravity will naturally pull the bubble down along the string.

9. As the bubble rolls down the string, tilt your hands the other direction. The bubble will roll the other way, too.

CABLE CAR BUBBLE

I got the idea for this when I was performing in Japan. I went on a cable car ride to the top of Mount Fuji and thought, "Hmm, I can make a cable car like this out of bubbles." So as soon as I got back to my hotel room, I cut off a piece of string, tried it...and sure enough, it worked.

Materials You'll Need
- A 4-foot piece of string.
- Bubble solution.
- A dish, bowl, or pan.

Tips: This is one where your hands have to be completely wet. No holding back.
- The bigger the bubble, the more impressive this trick looks.

Instructions

1. Blow a bubble into the air, the same as you did with the Tightrope Bubble (or have someone else do it). But this time, instead of blowing out the bubble film, leave it intact. This is important.

2. The string is now a cable car track. Catch the bubble on the track.

3. Stabilize it. Now turn it upside down, so the bubble is on the bottom side of the string, and it's a cable car.

4. By raising and lowering each end, you'll send the "cable car" up and down the track.

To make the bubble move faster down the track, open the lower end so it's wider than the top. It will go zipping down the string.

• As it gets to the bottom, open up the other side and tilt the string the other way—it'll zip down the other way, too.

• Conversely, if you make the lower end of the track narrower, then the bubble will slow down.

• Blow a bubble inside of the cable car bubble, and you've got a passenger.

BODY-SIZED BUBBLES

To most people, the idea of putting a person inside a bubble seems outrageous. But if you've already mastered everything else in this book, you should be able to do this trick with only a little practice.

Place: It must be done either outside when there's absolutely no wind, or in a basement with newspaper around.

Tip: This makes a bi-i-i-g mess.

Materials:
- A small children's swimming pool (should cost about $5 at a toy store).
- A hoop made out of 1/4-inch thick aluminum wire.
- Two gallons of bubble solution #3—the Industrial Strength kind.

Instructions
Before trying to make the bubble with a person inside, practice the bubble by itself.

1. Make a hoop 3 feet in diameter.

2. Wrap it with string—at least two wrappings, maybe three or four.

3. Pour an inch of bubble solution into the bottom of the pool.

4. Put the hoop down into the bubble solution. Make sure it's covered all the way around.

5. Bring the hoop straight up, making a gigantic soap bubble that's flat at the bottom (across the whole bottom of the pool).

6. With a twisting motion, break the bubble off at the top.

7. After you've mastered this, have a person step into the pool, and make the bubble around him or her.
- If the bubble touches the person, it'll pop.
- **Caution:** Standing in the bubble solution can be dangerous because the solution is very, very slippery!! It's more difficult to stand there than standing on ice. In fact, I build a platform for people to stand on, so they don't have to stand right in the solution. You might want to do that, too.

Mr. Bubbles' Tips:
Once you've got a hoop this big, you can make bubbles 8-10 feet in diameter.

When you're really good, you can put two people in a bubble at once.